Lost for Words

of related interest

Supporting Children in Public Care in Schools
A Resource for Trainers of Teachers, Carers and Social Workers
John Holland and Catherine Randerson
ISBN 1 84310 325 7

Understanding Children's Experiences of Parental Bereavement
John Holland
ISBN 1 84310 016 9

Without You
Children and Young People Growing Up with Loss and its Effects
Tamar Granot
ISBN 1 84310 297 8

Relative Grief
**Parents and children, sisters and brothers, husbands, wives and partners,
grandparents and grandchildren talk about their experience of death and grieving**
Clare Jenkins and Judy Merry
Foreword by Dorothy Rowe
ISBN 1 84310 257 9

Someone Very Important Has Just Died
**Immediate Help for People Caring for Children of All Ages
at the Time of a Close Bereavement**
Mary Turner
Illustrated by Elaine Bailey
ISBN 1 84310 295 1

Talking with Children and Young People about Death and Dying
A Workbook
Mary Turner
Illustrated by Bob Thomas
ISBN 1 85302 563 1

Helping Children to Manage Loss
Positive Strategies for Renewal and Growth
Brenda Mallon
ISBN 1 85302 605 0

The Forgotten Mourners, Second Edition
Guidelines for Working with Bereaved Children
Susan C. Smith
ISBN 1 85302 758 8

Grief in Children
A Handbook for Adults
Atle Dyregrov
ISBN 1 85302 113 X

Lost for Words

Loss and Bereavement Awareness Training

John Holland, Ruth Dance, Nic MacManus and Carole Stitt

Jessica Kingsley Publishers
London and Philadelphia

First published in 2005
by Jessica Kingsley Publishers
116 Pentonville Road
London N1 9JB, UK
and
400 Market Street, Suite 400
Philadelphia, PA 19106, USA

www.jkp.com

Library of Congress Cataloging in Publication Data

Lost for words : loss and bereavement awareness training / John Holland ... [et al.].— 1st American pbk. ed.
p. cm.
ISBN-13: 978-1-84310-324-0 (pbk.)
ISBN-10: 1-84310-324-9 (pbk.)
1. Loss (Psychology) in children. 2. Bereavement in children. 3. Grief in children. I. Holland, John, 1948-
BF723.L68L67 2005
155.9'37—dc22

2004026024

British Library Cataloguing in Publication Data
A CIP catalogue record for this book is available from the British Library

ISBN-13: 978 1 84310 324 0
ISBN-10: 1 84310 324 9

Printed and Bound in Great Britain by
Athenaeum Press, Gateshead, Tyne and Wear

I just did not know what to say; I was lost for words.

(Teacher talking about a bereaved child at his school)

Contents

1

Introduction

Lost for Words was developed from an idea by John Holland of the City Psychological Service, Learning and Cultural Services, Hull, together with colleagues Carole Stitt and Ruth Dance as well as Nic MacManus of the Hull-based Dove House Hospice: the team of four that deliver the training on a regular basis in Hull. Judith Hodgson, John Creasey and Janis Hostad, at the time of Dove House, were also involved in the development of the project. *Lost for Words* was launched in its original form in October 2000; this is the revised and well-tried version.

Lost for Words is a loss awareness training package for use with those working with children, especially in schools. The project developed from the collaborative multi-agency and multi-professional work carried out in the Hull area over many years. The professions involved included psychologists, educationalists, social workers and nurses.

Lost for Words is underpinned by research with bereaved children and their surviving parents as well as with schools, especially Operation Iceberg, a project carried out at the University of York.

The head teachers and staff of Hall Road Primary School and Newland St John's Church of England Primary School (both in the Hull local education authority) kindly allowed elements of the project to be trialled in training sessions at their schools. The project was also trialled on In-service Training (INSET) courses.

The aim of *Lost for Words* is to help teachers in schools to support pupils going through a bereavement because of death or other losses. *Lost for Words* is not a counselling training programme, nor does it address issues of trauma or abnormal grieving in depth.

The package is designed to be delivered by trainers, ideally in pairs, to staff in schools or in other settings. It comprises stand-alone topic areas and trainers can choose which are applicable to present in a particular context.

Resources are provided within the package, which is self-contained, including templates for overhead projector (OHP) transparencies. Guidance is also provided for trainers as well as handouts for trainees. These should be given out at the end of each session as appropriate. There is a book list providing references for further reading both for adults and children. Purchasers of the training package can photocopy material and make transparencies for an OHP. Please acknowledge the source of any material copied.

Ideally the course should be delivered on a training day or days. It can be used in whole, in part, or as a resource to dip into. It is suggested that Ice-breakers, Ground rules and Loss experience (Chapter 3, 4 and 6) are always included in any delivery.

Individuals will come to this training with a variety of life experiences. An assumption is made that the trainees are novices and that the trainers are aware of the general issues in the area of loss and have had some previous training and experience.

Those who have experienced a recent loss may find aspects of the course distressing and should be given the option, in good time, not to attend. Thought needs to be given as to how to support any trainees who find that the course does bring back painful and distressing personal memories. The training may also evoke similar memories for trainers.

For further information or ideas contact:

City Psychological Service
Learning Services
Kingston upon Hull City Council
2nd Floor, Essex House
Manor Street
Kingston upon Hull HU1 1YD
Tel: 01482 613390

2

Introducing trainees to the package

Careful consideration needs to be given to the size of the training group. The larger the group, the more inhibited trainees are likely to be about joining and fully engaging with the activities. An ideal group size is in the range of 8 to 16 members.

Much depends on the nature of the group. Staff may already be comfortable together, although they could equally be unwilling to share sensitive experiences.

Trainees should have been alerted to the nature of the course and had the opportunity to opt out if, for example, they have suffered a recent significant loss.

Individuals may find that the course brings back vivid memories of past experiences and the trainers need to give thought as to how to support trainees who become distressed. This may be quite unexpected. Trainees should be made to feel comfortable in being able to leave the room at any time and care should be taken to minimise any barriers between them and the door. If possible, a distressed trainee should be asked what would help and a trainer may need to offer them individual support.

Consideration needs to be given to seating arrangements. A circle or semi-circle of chairs may be better to encourage interaction than if the chairs are in rows. For some trainees this arrangement may initially be more threatening, although the ice-breakers may help to ameliorate this potentially difficult aspect.

The trainers could introduce themselves, explain the general purpose and aims of the course and then ask the trainees to introduce themselves individually. An alternative method would be to ask the trainees to speak briefly with a partner and then introduce each other to the group as a whole, in turn.

Closing down is an equally important activity. It may be helpful for the trainers to bring a session to a close by giving trainees the opportunities to share their thoughts about the session. The trainers should wait around after the session has finished in case there are issues that trainees wish to raise.

3

Ice-breakers

Introduction

Ice-breakers encourage the trainees to talk and to gain as much as possible from *Lost for Words* by actively engaging with the tasks. At least initially, trainees may be quite anxious about discussing issues of loss and death, especially in a group.

Aim

The aim is to help the trainees to engage quickly with the training.

Method of delivery

A list of suggested ice-breakers follows. These could be used with the trainees initially working together in pairs, perhaps then reporting back to the whole group. The chosen activity could depend on how well the trainees know each other.

1. *Something in common with a partner*
    Ask the trainees to talk with a partner and find something that they have in common. After five minutes, bring the group back together and ask the trainees to report briefly on their findings.

2. *Listening to your partner*
    Ask the trainees to talk about themselves with a partner who remains silent. Ask the trainees to swap roles after two minutes. Next bring the group together and ask the trainees to report briefly about their findings.

3. *Who would you like to have a 'one-to-one' with?*
    Ask the trainees each to find out from their partner whom they would like to talk to in a 'one-to-one' telephone conversation. After five minutes bring the group together and ask the trainees each to report briefly about their findings.

4. *Films seen recently*

   Ask the trainees to discuss in pairs a film that they have recently enjoyed. After five minutes bring the group together and ask the trainees each to report back briefly about their findings.

5. *Naming activity*

   Ask the trainees to say their names in turn, together with a brief statement about themselves. Using a soft or foam medium-size ball, the trainer starts a round by saying their name and throwing the ball to a trainee. This is repeated until all have been included, and can be varied by introducing other balls, and keeping the same pattern around the group.

6. *Something good*

   Ask the trainees to tell a partner about something good that has happened to them during that week. Ask the trainees to swap roles after two minutes. Next bring the group together and ask the trainees to report back briefly about their findings.

Materials

Three or four medium-size soft foam balls.

4

Ground rules

Introduction

Ideally the group should devise its own ground rules or ethos rather than having them imposed by the trainers. Ask the trainees for their ideas and record these on a flip chart or whiteboard.

If the group is unsure about what to include, or if time is short, then it is suggested that the trainers provide guidance. Transparency 1 could be used here as a stimulus for a group discussion.

Areas for consideration could include:

- confidentiality within the group

- any 'opt-out' possibilities for exercises

- respecting all contributions made by members

- a culture of caring

- group members actively listening to each other

- group members having the option to leave the session.

Bereavement is a sensitive area. Things may arise from the past that bring back perhaps forgotten memories, and care does need to be taken when presenting the package.

Materials

- Flip chart or whiteboard and pens

- Overhead projector (OHP)

- Transparency 1.

✓

Ground rules

- Confidentiality

- 'Opt-outs'

- Caring

- Listening

5

Research

Introduction

Lost for Words is underpinned by research in schools, and also with adults bereaved of a parent when of school age. The research is partly drawn from Operation Iceberg, a doctoral research project at the University of York, involving a survey of nearly 100 volunteers. Most of these were bereaved of a parent when they were children. The research is intended to alert trainees to the potential difficulties faced by children, especially at school, after a parental bereavement.

Method of delivery

Show the trainees Transparency 2. This shows how the children taking part in Operation Iceberg felt on their return to school after a parental bereavement. These are generally not positive statements, but do show the importance of the transition back to school after a death or significant loss.

Transparency 3 shows the children's perceptions of their schools' response to their bereavement. Generally the children felt that their school had not responded at all. This may be different from the perception of the school, but to be effective a response needs to be seen as such.

Transparency 4 shows that nearly three-quarters of the children did not find teachers approachable.

Transparency 5 shows that the majority of children did not speak in any depth to anybody at all about the death of their parent. This has echoes of the isolation of bereaved children on their return to school shown in Transparency 2.

Transparency 6 shows that all the children held the view that their school had not helped them to prepare for the bereavement.

Transparency 7 shows that nearly half of the children felt that school had not helped them during the bereavement.

This research underpins the *Lost for Words* pack, and shows in terms of the research findings how bereaved children could be best supported.

Materials

- OHP

- Transparencies 2 to 7.

Further reading

Holland, J. (2001) *Understanding Children's Experiences of Parental Bereavement.* London: Jessica Kingsley Publishers.

Feelings on the return to school

- Ignored

- Isolated

- Normal

- Embarrassed

- No memory

- Uncertain

- Different

The school response

- Nothing (67%)

- One teacher spoke (11%)

- Primed peers (10%)

- No recall (4%)

- Tolerant (3%)

- Gave normality (3%)

✓

Were teachers approachable?

- No (74%)

- Didn't want to approach them (6%)

- One teacher 'OK' (4%)

- Yes (4%)

- No recall (4%)

✓

Who children spoke to about their feelings

- Nobody (56%)

- Close friends (20%)

- Siblings (13%)

- Mother (11%)

- Grandmother (4%)

- Family friend (3%)

- Father (3%)

✓

Did school help them prepare for the bereavement?

- No (100%)

- Yes (0%)

✓

Did their school help
with the bereavement?

- No (44%)

- Gave normality (24%)

- Neutral (12%)

- 'OK' (9%)

6

Loss experience

Introduction

Individuals may find the whole subject of loss quite difficult and also not connect the theory of loss with their own personal experiences. Loss is on a continuum from small to great and this chapter is intended to engage the trainees in considering the loss of an object rather than the breaking of a bond with a person. The range of emotions experienced may be quite similar but at a less intense level.

Aim

The loss experience helps the trainees to consider the area of loss in a non-threatening way and gives them an insight into the range of emotions covered by loss. Two alternative exercises are provided:

1.   Losing a favourite thing.
2.   Losing a friend's bike.

Losing a favourite thing

Method of delivery

Ask the trainees to imagine losing a favourite or sentimental personal item, such as a watch. Then ask them to imagine how they would feel at the following times:

- at the time of the loss
- after two weeks
- after six months
- after two years.

Show the trainees Transparency 8 to remind them of the time periods. Ask pairs of trainees to discuss their likely feelings at the various times and then report these back to the group.

The trainer could record these feelings on a flip chart or whiteboard, using this information later to draw a connection with the models of loss (Chapter 9).

Transparency 9 could then be used to show the trainees a potential range of emotions felt after a loss. The point could then be made that there are many shared and similar feelings after any loss.

Materials

- Flip chart or whiteboard and pens

- OHP

- Transparencies 8 and 9

- Handout 1.

Losing a friend's bike

Method of delivery

Prepare two balloons, writing on them some of the feelings from Transparency 9. Keep the balloons hidden from the trainees, one inflated and kept in the bag. The 'Stolen Bike' story sheet can either be read to the trainees or improvised around the 'core items' below. Before telling the story, ask the trainees to focus on their feelings during the story, trying to put themselves in the position of the boy.

Core items to the story

- A friend lends you a new and expensive bike.

- You ride into a remote area 'to get away from it all'.

- You rest the bike against a fence and walk into a wood.

- You decide to return home as it is getting dark and the weather is becoming stormy.

- You find that the bike has been stolen.

- There are no houses in sight and you are unsure of the way home.

Tell the trainees the story then ask them to brainstorm their feelings. Write these feelings down on a flip chart or whiteboard.

Next show the trainees the inflated balloon. Pass it around the group and ask the trainees to comment on the feelings written on the balloon. Ask them how you knew which feelings to write on the balloon. Make the point that there are many shared and similar feelings after any loss.

Ask the trainees how the balloon feels to the touch, in particular its fragility and vulnerability. It could easily burst with a 'bang'. Then, after checking that nobody minds, burst the balloon with a pin. Ask the trainees if it can be repaired.

Then bring out the second balloon. Blow it up and ask the trainees how the balloon can be deflated safely. Deflate it gently, pointing out the way in which the 'feelings' written on the balloon shrink, and yet become clearer. The feelings shrink, but do not disappear.

The first balloon burst with only the slightest point of a pin. Equate deflating the balloon with talking about feelings, releasing them safely. Transparency 9 could be shown here. Ask the trainees if they could think of other ways that feelings can be released by adults and children. These could include:

- talking
- artistic expression
- painting
- music
- drama
- writing.

Teaching points

- Events in life generate feelings – this is normal, not going mad.
- These feelings are generated in us all.
- We need to acknowledge that our feelings are sometimes bad and negative.
- Sadness is not the only emotion when we 'lose' something or someone.
- Action has to be taken to prevent the 'blow-out'.
- Whose responsibility is it to take this action?
- Action removes the hierarchy of loss. It is not 'worse' to lose one thing rather than another – it depends on the individual and their attachment.

Materials

- Flip chart or whiteboard and pens
- OHP
- Transparency 9
- Two balloons and pins (condoms are an alternative!)
- A large laundry bag
- Story: The Stolen Bike
- Handout 1.

Story: The Stolen Bike by John Creasey, March 1992

It was a beautiful afternoon. The sun was shining and the birds were singing. As I walked up the street to Dave's house, I thought how wonderful it would be to get out of the town and into the country for the afternoon. Mam and Dad couldn't afford to buy me a bike and I couldn't afford the bus fare. I could only dream about riding into the open spaces.

As I turned into Dave's drive I was met by a huge grin from Dave as he shouted, 'Do you like me new bike Steve?' I looked in amazement at his brand new and very expensive bike, the kind that I could only dream about. I could have felt so jealous, but Dave was me best mate and he was always really good with me. We'd been mates all the way through school together.

I told Dave that I'd just been wishing that I had a bike to get out into the freedom of the country for a while. 'I'll tell you what,' he said, 'I'm going with me mam into town in a few minutes, why don't you borrow it for the afternoon.' At first I couldn't accept, but Dave insisted and so, full of excitement, I pedalled off towards the country.

Oh, it was brill! I felt fantastic in the warm, fresh air. Mile after mile I pedalled. I had no idea where I was going as I'd never been out this way before. Everything was new. I began to get tired after a while. Anyway, me bum was sore from the saddle. I decided to take a break somewhere down this long windy road that seemed miles from anywhere. I hadn't seen another person or house for what seemed ages.

I came across a little wood and decided I would explore it a bit. I leant Dave's bike up against the fence and walked back into the trees. It was fantastic! After a while, I lay down on my back looking upwards into the sun gently coming through the tops of the trees as they swayed in the gentle breeze.

I didn't know how long I'd been there, but I could tell it was getting darker. I decided that it was time to go home, so made my way back out of the wood. As I did so, I heard the rumble of thunder in the distance. Coming into the clearing, I could see lightning flashing in the distance and the sky getting really dark, as the night and the storm clouds fast approached.

Phew! I knew that it was time to scarper back home as things looked really bad, so I hastened over to the fence to get back on the bike...it was gone!!!!

[PAUSE]

I suddenly realised that no one knew where I was. They wouldn't know where to find me and it was ages since I'd seen a house in which to shelter. Soon it would be totally dark and I wouldn't even be able to see the familiar landmarks that would help me find my way home.

Losing a favourite thing

- At the time of the loss

- After two weeks

- After six months

- After two years

Loss feelings

- Anger
- Blame
- Guilt
- Sadness
- Shock
- Confusion
- Relief
- Horror
- Disbelief

- Anxiety
- Depression
- Frustration
- Distress
- Unhappiness
- Worry
- Irritability
- Fear
- Abandonment

Handout 1: Loss experience

- The subject of loss may be one that is quite difficult, especially around the area of bereavement or loss through the death of a loved one. However, we may not connect the theory of loss with our own personal experiences and emotions.

- The experience of loss events can generate many feelings; this is a normal feature of life. Sadness is not the only emotion that we experience when we 'lose' something or somebody. Other feelings may include: anger, blame, guilt, shock, confusion, relief, horror, disbelief, anxiety, depression, frustration, distress, unhappiness, upset, worry, shame.

- Loss is on a continuum from small to great. There is no definitive hierarchy of loss and it is not 'worse' to lose one thing rather than another. The feelings experienced will depend on the individual and the degree of attachment to the thing or person that has been lost. The range of emotions experienced in any loss may be quite similar but may be felt at a less intense level.

- It seems to help if feelings are expressed, although not everybody finds this an easy thing to do. Death is not encountered as frequently as in our recent past and there may not be the family support systems of the past with families perhaps now more geographically dispersed.

7

Changes

Introduction

We all face changes throughout life. These can be positive or negative, wanted or unwanted, anticipated or unexpected. Many of these changes will involve gains. There may also be losses, even in the case of apparently positive change such as a. marriage or birth.

Aim

The exercises are intended to widen the trainees' awareness of the concept of loss by reflecting on their own life experiences. Two activities are provided in this section and one or both could be used:

1. Life line.

2. Age and loss experience.

Time line

Aim

The outcome of this exercise should be that the trainees realise that they have all experienced both positive and negative experiences throughout their lives and that there is a subjective value attached to each experience.

Method of delivery

Give each trainee a 'life line' handout which has been photocopied from Transparency 10. Ask the trainees to focus on a 20-year period of their life and to think about significant changes that took place within that time. Positive experiences are recorded above the axis and negative ones below.

Next ask the trainees to allocate a score for up to eight of the events (four positive and four negative events) taken from their life line. Use a scale of 1 to 10, with 1 being the most negative and 10 the most positive effect of the event.

Bring the group together for a discussion but be aware that some may not wish to share parts of their life line. The trainer should draw from what is shared to make the point that we all experience losses and gains over time and we attach a subjective value to each of these experiences.

Materials

- Flip chart or whiteboard and pens
- OHP
- Transparency 10
- Handout copied from Transparency 10
- Handout 2.

Age and loss experience

Aim

The outcome of this exercise should be the realisation that individuals experience different types of change and loss throughout their lives. These will vary depending on their age and the context of their lives.

Method of delivery

Divide the trainees into three groups. Ask one group to discuss and record the loss situations likely to be faced by a young child. Ask the second group to consider the possible changes faced by an adolescent, and the third group to consider the possible changes faced by an adult.

After ten minutes, ask the groups to come together to compare and discuss their findings. Record these findings on a flip chart.

Show the group Transparency 11, summarising some of the losses which individuals may have experienced within either activity. This could form the basis of a group discussion.

Materials

- Flip chart or whiteboard and pens
- OHP
- Transparency 11
- A large sheet of paper for each group
- Handout 2.

My life line

10

+

−

0

On a scale of 1 to 10, 1 has the least impact and 10 has the most.

Positive event	Score		Negative event	Score

Handout 2: Our own changes

We all face changes throughout life. These can be positive or negative, wanted or unwanted, anticipated or unexpected. Many of these changes will involve gains. There may also be losses, even in the case of apparently positive change such as a marriage. An initial first-level change, such as parental death, may lead to further changes: for example, children having to move area, or school, and losing contact with their friends, classmates and family members. Other changes include:

- starting or leaving school and college

- losing a favourite toy or possession

- changing schools or classes

- birth or death of a sibling, relation or significant other

- relationship breakdowns, divorce or separation

- leaving home

- starting, changing or leaving jobs

- physical or mental difficulties

- amputation

- accident or illness

- imprisonment

- homelessness or refugee status.

Other losses

- Pet
- Friendship
- Marriage
- Home
- Starting/leaving school/college/class
- Innocence
- Community
- Parent
- Faith
- Possessions
- Freedom
- Children
- Divorce/separation
- Retirement
- Self-identity

- Birth of sibling
- Security
- Disability
- Relationship
- Stability
- Illness
- Mental health
- Emigration
- Having special educational needs
- Limb
- Dreams
- Culture
- Self-worth
- Sense of belonging

8

Case study

Aim

The case study is an alternative method of engaging the trainees in considering the wider issues affecting children after the death of a parent.

Method of delivery

Divide the trainees into pairs. Ask the trainees to read the case study shown on Transparency 12 and to identify as many losses as possible.

After ten minutes, ask the trainees to come together to compare and discuss their findings. Record these findings on a flip chart.

Show the group Transparency 13, summarising some of the losses which the child may have experienced. This could form the basis of a group discussion.

Materials

- Flip chart or whiteboard and pens
- OHP
- Transparencies 12 and 13
- Handout 2.

Tim's story

Tim is 10 years old and used to attend his local neighbour-hood city school with 400 children on roll. He lived near his paternal grandparents. Tim played in the school band and football team, and had two best friends, Ken and Dave. Tim and his dad had a season ticket for the local premier-ship football team. Tim's dad was killed in an accident at work. Tim's mother, who does not drive, was unable to keep the family home and they moved 150 miles away to live with her brother on an arable farm in a small hamlet. The village school has 30 children on roll.

Tim's changes

- Dad

- Ken and Dave

- School

- Classmates

- Teachers

- House

- Neighbourhood

- Subculture

- Hobbies

- Grandparents

- Urban environment

9

Models of loss

Introduction

Humans are social animals and the making of bonds helps group cohesion. Whenever significant bonds are broken there will be a grief reaction, the level of which depends on the context and the significance of the loss. Grieving relates to the experience of loss in general, death being only one type of loss. For simplicity, the focus is on three approaches that are described briefly:

1. Grieving as a passive experience

2. Grieving as an active experience

3. Grieving as an ongoing experience

The models all offer 'pegs' onto which the trainees can hang personal experiences of loss and may, or may not, reflect the individual's own experiences.

Aim

This provides the trainees with a simplified theoretical background to help them to relate and make sense of their own personal experiences.

Method of delivery

Introduce the topic by showing the trainees Transparency 14 that gives an overview of three models.

Next, show the trainees the transparencies in the sequence outlined in the following sections, also making a connection with the previous loss exercise (Chapter 6). The emotional experiences shown in each model should relate directly to those feelings reported by the trainees in that exercise.

Materials

- Flip chart or whiteboard and pens

- OHP

- Transparencies 14 to 20

- Handout 3.

Passive model of loss

The attention of the trainees should be drawn to the passive or stage model of grieving, based on Kübler-Ross (1980) and is shown on Transparency 15. Here the bereaved person passes through a series of stages from the initial experience of the loss or death, to the final resolution of grief. The stages of the model shown on Transparency 15 include:

- shock and denial

- separation and pain

- guilt and anger

- sadness

- final resolution and acceptance.

Individuals are often in a state of shock after first hearing the news of a loss and they may also deny that the event has happened. Feelings of pain and separation may naturally flow as the reality of the loss is realised. Individuals may also have feelings of guilt: for example, they may blame themselves for an act or omission that may have altered the course of events and either prevented or caused the loss. This could include feelings of regret. The bereaved may also be angry with others, such as the medical services, and attribute blame for this loss.

With time, these may be replaced with feelings of sadness or even depression. Eventually, for most people the loss will finally be accepted or resolved. For a minority, including children, individuals may be 'stuck' at a particular stage and need the help of outside agencies.

Show the trainees Transparency 16, which visually represents the model in cartoon form. The train is shown moving through the 'track' of grieving. The train calls at different stations along the way, representing the stages of grieving, with the journey ending at the destination of resolution or the acceptance of the loss. In this model the individual is a passive passenger in the train.

Active model of loss

The trainees' attention should be drawn to the active or task model of grieving, based on Worden (1991) and shown on Transparency 17. In this model the bereaved has actively to complete a series of tasks before the loss is finally resolved or accepted. The bereaved has to:

- initially accept the reality of the loss

- feel the pain of the separation

- adjust to the loss

- finally invest his or her emotional energy elsewhere.

After a loss, the first task is for the individual to accept the reality of the loss. Here, rituals and rites such as seeing the body or attending a funeral can help. Individuals may go through feelings of pain and separation after a loss and this is quite normal. Eventually they will adjust to the loss in their life and finally invest their emotional energy elsewhere, withdrawing it from the deceased. This is similar to the notion of acceptance in the passive model, although here the bereaved takes a more active role.

Show the trainees Transparency 18, a visual representation in cartoon form of the active model. The train is shown moving through the 'track' of grieving, calling at the different stations representing the tasks. The journey ends when the individual has completed the final task of investing emotional energy elsewhere. In this model the individual is actively driving the train to the final destination.

Continuing bonds model of loss

The trainees' attention should be drawn to the continuing bonds model, which is shown on Transparency 19, based on, for example, Silverman's model (Klass, Silverman and Nickman 1996). The bereaved retains a continuing but changing relationship with that which is lost. Here, there is no notion of resolution or acceptance, but the relationship unfolds over time, and there is a growing and changing awareness depending on the age and stage of the bereaved. Other cultures and previous past generations would have been quite comfortable with the idea that the link with the past is unbroken and that a relationship continues. The idea of 'detachment' or the total severing of links with the deceased as being healthy is a relatively contemporary notion. The bereaved has:

- a continuing relationship with the deceased

- 'detachment' from the deceased

- a changing relationship with the deceased over time

- no 'resolution' of the loss.

Next show the trainees Transparency 20, a visual representation in cartoon form of the continuing bonds model. Here, the train does not have a final destination, and the relationship with that which is lost remains. The individual is also driving the train.

Further reading

Klass, D., Silverman, P.R. and Nickman, S.L. (1996) *Continuing Bonds, New Understandings of Grief.* London: Taylor and Francis (Continuing Bonds Model).

Kübler-Ross, E. (1980) *On Death and Dying.* London: Tavistock/Routledge (Stage Model).

Worden, J.W. (1991) *Grief Counselling and Grief Therapy.* Tavistock/Routledge (Task Model).

Models of Loss

- Passive

- Active

- Continuing bonds

TRANSPARENCY 14

Passive Model of Loss

- Shock and denial

- Separation and pain

- Guilt and anger

- Sadness

- Resolution

Passive Model of Loss

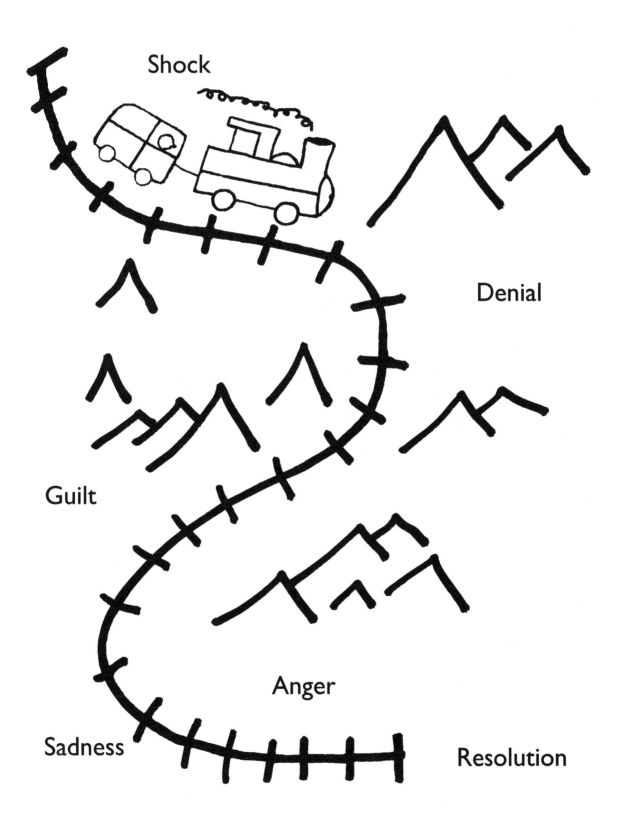

Shock

Denial

Guilt

Anger

Sadness

Resolution

✓

Active Model of Loss

- Accept the reality

- Feel the pain

- Adjust to the loss

- Invest emotional energy elsewhere

Active Model of Loss

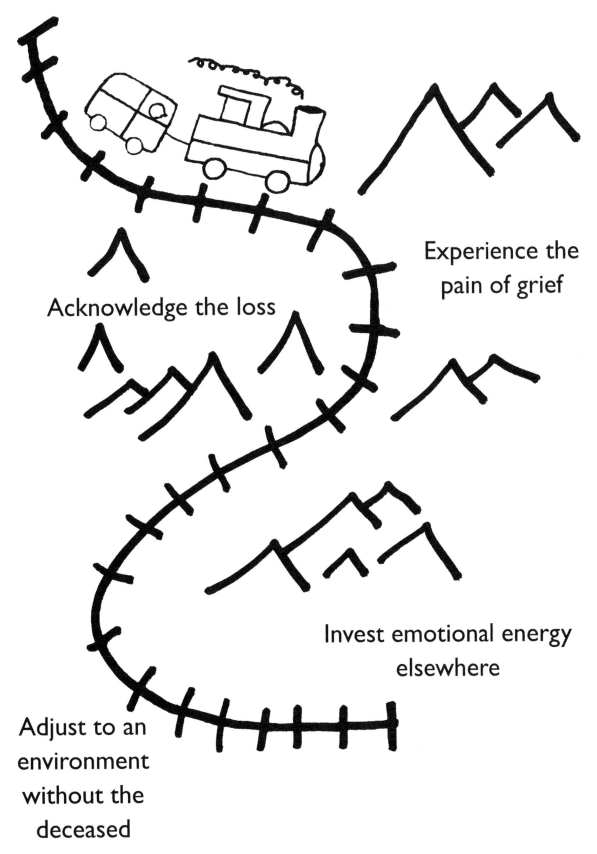

Acknowledge the loss

Experience the pain of grief

Invest emotional energy elsewhere

Adjust to an environment without the deceased

Continuing Bonds Model of Loss

- Has a continuing relationship

- Does not 'detach'

- Has a changing relationship

- There is no 'resolution'

Continuing Bonds Model of Loss

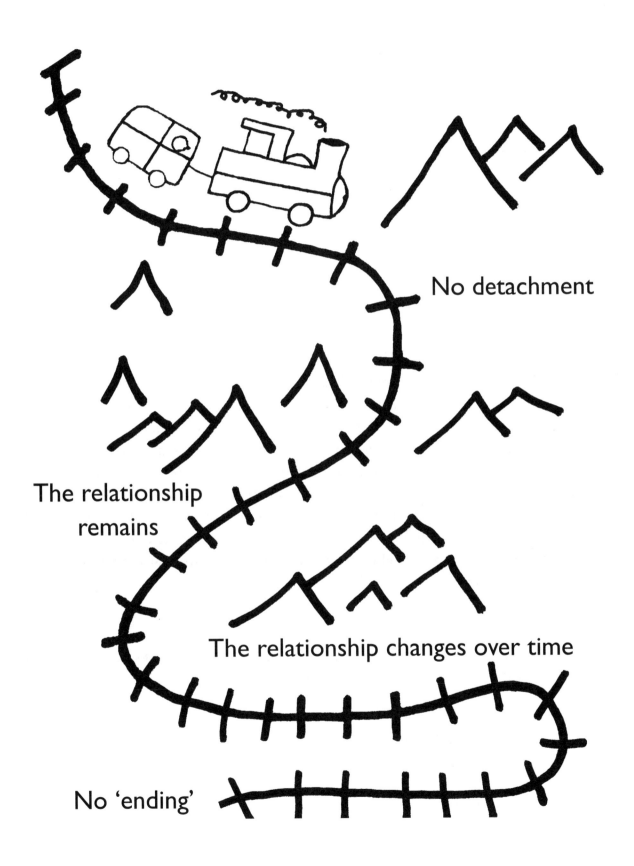

No detachment

The relationship remains

The relationship changes over time

No 'ending'

Handout 3: Models of loss

Humans are social animals and the making of these bonds helps to develop group cohesion. When these bonds are broken we may have a grief reaction, the level of which depends on the context and the significance of the loss. The different models should be seen as 'pegs' on which to hang concepts and experiences.

1. Passive model

The bereaved person passes through a series of stages from the initial experience of the loss or death to final resolution of grief:

- shock and denial

- separation and pain

- guilt and anger

- sadness

- final resolution and acceptance.

Individuals are often in a state of shock after first hearing the news of a loss and may also deny that the event has happened. Feelings of pain and separation may naturally flow as the reality of the loss is realised. They may also have feelings of guilt: for example, blaming themselves for an act or omission that may have altered the course of events or even prevented or caused the loss. This could include regrets. They may also be angry with others such as the medical services and attach outside blame for this loss. In time, these feelings may be replaced with feelings of sadness or even depression. Eventually, for most people the loss will be finally accepted or resolved. For a minority, including some children, they may be 'stuck' at a particular stage and need the help of outside agencies.

2. Active model

In this model, the bereaved have actively to complete a series of tasks before their grief is finally resolved or the loss accepted. They should:

- initially accept the reality of the loss

- feel the pain of separation

- adjust to the loss

- finally invest his or her emotional energy elsewhere.

After a loss the first task is for the individual to accept the reality of the loss. Here, rituals and rites such as seeing the body or attending a funeral can help. Individuals will go through feelings of pain and separation after a loss and this is quite normal. Eventually they will adjust to the loss in their life and finally invest their emotional energy elsewhere, withdrawing it from the deceased.

3. Continuing bonds model

In this model there is no 'detachment' from the deceased, but a relationship, which remains over time. The bereaved has:

- a continuing relationship with the deceased

- no 'detachment' from the deceased

- a changing relationship with the deceased over time

- no 'resolution' of the loss.

The idea of this model is that the bereaved retains a continuing but changing relationship with that which has been lost. There is no notion of resolution or acceptance in this model, but the relationship unfolds over time.

Other cultures and previous generations would have been quite comfortable with the idea that the link with the past is unbroken and that a relationship continues. The idea of 'detachment' or total severing of links as being healthy or necessary to 'move on' is a relatively contemporary notion.

10

Children's understanding of death

Introduction

Children's understanding of death will depend on their age and cognitive level as well as their previous experience. For simplicity, the focus is on three main stages:

- 0 to 4 years: emergent understanding

- 4 to 8 years: limited understanding

- 7 to 16+ years: fuller understanding.

Aim

The outcome of this exercise should be the realisation that an individual's understanding of death relates to age and experience.

Method of delivery

Ask pairs of trainees to spend two or three minutes looking at handouts prepared from Transparency 21. Ask the trainees to match the statements to the age groups, including the 'Unlikely' box. Bring the group back together for feedback and discussion.

There are no absolutely correct answers to this exercise. Complex language is more likely to be used by older children, as are statements indicating a more complex understanding of death.

Next show the trainees Transparency 22 with the three main stages of children's understanding of death:

- 0 to 4 years: emergent

- 4 to 8 years: limited

- 7 to 16+ years: fuller

Alert the trainees to the simplified three stages of understanding, from no concept at all to an adult understanding. Trainers may have their own experiences to relate here. For example, children may wish that somebody was dead because their needs were denied. If the person then actually dies, children may believe through magical thinking that they have caused the death.

Materials

- Flip chart or whiteboard and pens
- OHP
- Transparencies 21 and 22
- Handout produced from Transparency 21
- Handout 4.

Children's understanding of death

Scenario

Mary is 35 years old and has three children aged 3, 6 and 13 years. Mary dies suddenly at work from a heart attack. Match with a line the age of the children with the statements they are likely to have made. Some of the statements may be unlikely to have been said by any of the age groups!

3 years	• Who will now be feeding Mum?
	• Everybody eventually dies
6 years	• Mummy died because I ate her sweeties
13 years	• Me deaded Mummy
	• All Mummy people die in end
Unlikely	• When's Mum coming home?

Age and the understanding of death

- 0 to 4 years: emergent

- 4 to 8 years: limited

- 7 to 16+ years: fuller

Handout 4: Children's understanding of death

Stage 1: 0 to 4 years

Until about 2 years of age, children respond to separation from a close attachment figure without necessarily grasping the long-term implications i.e. that the person is not coming back. At around the age of 2, children do not understand the permanence of separation and tend to think in literal terms. Therefore, the type of language used should be clear rather than euphemistic. It is not uncommon for children to ask about the physical well-being of the dead person and they may seem to take things in their stride, frequently asking for their toys and possessions. Children may build up fantasies far worse than the reality if they are not given the facts from adults who are trying to protect them.

Stage 2: 4 to 8 years

As children develop intellectually and emotionally, they become more aware that death has a cause, cannot be reversed and may happen to anyone. Their language develops and as a result their cognitive understanding is greater, but they may still be literal in their thinking. In order to deal with the difficult situation, some children may use their imagination and 'magical thinking' to make things feel safe. They may feel responsible for the death, believing that their destructive fantasies may have come true, e.g. 'wishing someone dead'. As a result they may feel that the death is a form of punishment to them for doing something wrong.

Stage 3: 7 years to adult

From 7 or 8 years of age onwards, most children have an adult understanding of death, but some may still see death as a form of punishment and there may still be signs of magical thinking. Their own future death becomes more of a reality. During the adolescent stage their concept of death becomes more abstract and they understand more of the long-term consequences of loss. This stage may be characterised by anxieties although many just get on with life. However, significant losses may cause regression to a previous stage of development. It is important to consider children's level of understanding in addition to their chronological age.

11

Euphemisms

Introduction

Euphemisms are most frequently used for taboo subjects such as death as a way of avoiding talking about the subject. Although adults will be aware of the double meaning attached to euphemisms, children, especially younger ones or those with language difficulties, may either be confused or take the euphemism literally. Although a belief may be involved, such as 'gone to heaven', it is the language used to communicate this that may confuse children. For example, children may think that relatives have literally 'gone to sleep' or been 'taken by Jesus'. This may lead to the fear of sleeping or of going to church. Care needs to be taken when communicating with young people to explain things clearly in terms which they can understand.

Aim

The outcome of this exercise should be the raising of awareness of the potential difficulties of using euphemisms and the confusion that these may cause.

Method of delivery

The trainees should be shown Transparency 23 showing two common euphemisms for death in cartoon form. This could be used to generate discussion around the use of language. Ask the trainees to think of other euphemisms.

This activity could either be completed as a group brainstorm, or used as a homework activity, with feedback the following session. Transparency 24, which gives some examples of common euphemisms, can be shown to the trainees.

Materials

- Flip chart or whiteboard and pens
- OHP
- Transparencies 23 and 24
- Handout 5.

Euphemisms

- Snuffed it

- Kicked the bucket

- Gone to sleep

- Passed away/on

- Popped his clogs

- Crossed over

- Pushing up daisies

- Lost

- Taken by Jesus

- Gone to heaven

- Gone to live with the angels

- Gone to meet his Maker

- Put him/her down

- At the happy hunting ground

Handout 5: Euphemisms

- Euphemisms are most frequently used for taboo topics, such as death, as a way of avoiding talking about the subject. They may be a way of softening or of avoiding the use of the word 'death'. Although adults will be aware of the double meaning attached to euphemisms, children may not understand and either take things literally or be quite confused.

- We need to take care when communicating with young people, to explain things clearly in terms that they can understand.

- Euphemisms may lead to confusion and misunderstanding for young people, especially for those either at the literal or concrete stage of cognitive development, or on the autistic spectrum. They can cause difficulties if they are misconstrued by children. If, for example, an adult says that the dead person has 'gone to sleep', then the child may take this literally and be fearful of going to sleep. Children may think that a relative has been 'taken by Jesus'. This may make children fear going to church, in case they too 'are taken'. The use of other euphemisms such as 'lost' may equally confuse youngsters.

- Young children will be building up their own internal models of loss and death, which may be confused by euphemisms.

- It is important to liaise closely with the family on this issue and check what the children have been told.

12

Death as taboo

Introduction

Death happens to us all, yet seems to be a subject often avoided or ignored in conversation on a personal level. We do not seem to have the same difficulty with death presented in the media, which usually present death as violent, traumatic or speedy. This contrasts with most 'real-life' deaths, but may mean that we develop a stereotyped view of death related to these media images.

Aim

The trainees will gain greater insight into the reasons why death may be a taboo subject. Although death can be taboo, it may be easier to discuss in general terms. For example, death observed in the media is remote and there are no bonds with the deceased. This contrasts with the death of someone with whom there was a close relationship.

Method of delivery

Show the trainees Transparency 25 and ask them to discuss in pairs and give reasons as to how comfortable or otherwise they think that they would be in speaking about death in the following three circumstances:

- in general terms

- to someone who is dying

- to someone who is bereaved.

Then bring the group back together and discuss the trainees' thoughts, feelings and reasoning. Record these on a flip chart or whiteboard, divided into the three areas of discussion.

Materials

- Flip chart or whiteboard and pens

- OHP

- Transparency 25.

Death as taboo

Consider whether you find it easy or difficult to speak about death:

- generally

- to someone who is terminally ill

- to a bereaved person

Handout 6: Death as taboo

Death happens to us all, yet is a subject that seems far easier to discuss on a general rather than a personal level. Some of the following may also be factors as to why discussion of death at a personal level is often difficult:

- Death in the media is usually presented as being violent, traumatic or speedy. This image may relate to a news story, which may involve disaster and trauma in order to be 'newsworthy'. This contrasts with most 'real-life' deaths, but may mean that we develop a stereotyped view of death relating to the media image rather than the reality.

- Death is not usually encountered on a personal level as frequently as in times past, or in some other cultures outside our western world.

- Science has reduced the incidence of infant mortality and there is also a greater expectation that technology will save us.

- There is a general reduction in religious belief such as in an afterlife. Death may now be seen as a final event rather than moving on to 'better things', and hence is a more difficult subject.

- Families now tend to be separated by distance and there may not be the same support systems as in the past.

There is a decline in the rituals surrounding death. Often, only the funeral remains as a vestige of a former time where there was a complex response to a death in terms of mourning rites. These perhaps gave both greater support to the bereaved and more certainty to those with whom they interact.

13

Changes in learning and behaviour

Introduction

Changes in behaviour may be an expression of the range of emotions being experienced by children after a significant loss. A pupil presenting with behaviour difficulties may, for example, be going through the loss reaction of anger. A pupil whose attainments have declined could be so preoccupied with the loss that they find concentrating difficult. Individual variations include:

- the context of the loss

- the degree of attachment

- peaks and troughs of the intensity of grief

- individual experiences and construction of the loss.

Individuals may:

- act out of character

- lose self-esteem

- have disturbed sleep patterns

- be susceptible to illness and minor accidents

- lose concentration

- revert to an earlier developmental stage

- experience a change in academic performance.

Aim

The outcome of this exercise should be the realisation by the trainees that changes in behaviour and learning can lead directly and indirectly from a loss.

Method of delivery

Ask pairs of trainees to discuss the potential effects that a loss may have on pupils at school. The trainees should be reminded of their previous loss experience and also of the models of loss, and that many behaviours relate to the emotions and feelings being experienced after a loss. Ask the trainees to consider the areas of emotion, health, academic and social. A transparency relating to the potential social effects for asylum seekers is included to be used if relevant.

After ten minutes, bring the group together for feedback. Write the experiences on a flip chart or whiteboard and compare these with Transparencies 26 to 30 which have the 'markers' shown under the following headings:

1.   Emotional

2.   Physical

3.   Academic

4.   Social

5.   Social (asylum seekers).

Transparencies 31 and 32 show issues that were raised in the Operation Iceberg study, and can be shown as specific examples of difficulties reported.

The trainees need to be alerted to the idea that most pupils will not need specialist help, especially if they are provided with initial help as suggested in Chapter 14, Helping children. A small percentage of pupils may need to be referred elsewhere. The warning signs and the potential helping agencies are located in Chapter 20, Helping agencies.

Materials

- Flip chart or whiteboard and pens

- OHP

- Transparencies 26 to 32

- Handout 7.

Emotional markers

- Mood swings

- Anger

- Withdrawal

- Forgetfulness

- Aggression

- Violence

- Loss of self-esteem

- Regression

- Clinginess

- Attention seeking

- Depression

Physical markers

- Sleep problems/nightmares

- Headaches

- Skin disorders

- Bowel and stomach problems

- Psychosomatic illnesses

- Vulnerability to accidents

- Bedwetting

- Depressed immune system

✓

Academic markers

- Poor concentration

- Restlessness

- Truanting

- Poor punctuality

- Lowered expectations

- Change in attainments

- Disorganisation

- Loss of interest

- School refusal

✓

Social markers

- Substance abuse

- Criminal activity

- Clinical depression

- Promiscuity

- Isolation

- Suicide

- Gambling

- Prostitution

- Vulnerability

Social markers (asylum seekers)

- Cultural confusion

- Community isolation

- Language difficulties

- Violent behaviour

- Withdrawal

- Friendship difficulties

- Effects of trauma

Operation Iceberg study issues (1)

- Deterioration in school work and behaviour

- School refusal

- Depression

- Withdrawal

- Attention seeking

- Substance abuse

Operation Iceberg study issues (2)

- Truancy

- Being on criminal fringes

- Deterioration in school work and behaviour

- The return to school is a key response time

Handout 7: Changes in learning and behaviour

- Changes in young people's behaviour may be an expression of the range of emotions, such as anger or depression experienced by them after a loss. Most young people will eventually work through these feelings in socially acceptable ways, although some may become involved in antisocial behaviour such as crime or substance abuse. The majority of pupils will not need referring for specialist help. Young people may well need time, space and support from the adults in their lives to help them through this period.

- There will be variations in the length of time that young people will be affected by their loss, depending on factors such as the context of the loss and the degree of their attachment. There may well be peaks and troughs of emotions as individuals work through these issues.

- Losses are an essentially individual experience and assumptions cannot be made about the degree to which they will affect children. The death of a pet, for example, may be a major and significant loss for an individual. A pupil may outwardly appear to be coping or unmoved, but this may not reflect his or her true internal state and feelings.

- Individuals may also act out of character at a time of loss. There may be loss of self-esteem, disturbed sleep patterns and a susceptibility to illness and minor accidents through concentration loss. Youngsters may revert to an earlier developmental stage, for example, sucking their thumb or bedwetting. Academic performance may also be affected, either by a decline or less commonly by an improvement. Young people may throw themselves with enthusiasm into academic work as a way of coping with or escaping from their loss.

- These behaviour changes may present over a period of time, even years after the loss event. Transitions between classes and schools are important and communication is a key element. Teachers and other adults at school may need to be made aware of individual circumstances. Most students will not need specialist help, but a small percentage may need to be referred elsewhere.

14

Helping children

Introduction

It is important to consider the needs of children and their families after a loss and how this may impact on many aspects of school life including behaviour, learning and attendance. After a loss children may lack:

- information about the loss

- control over events, for example attending a funeral

- understanding about what is happening.

Aim

The outcome of this exercise should be a greater awareness of how death or loss may be experienced by children and how they may be helped in the context of school.

Method of delivery

Show the trainees Transparency 33, explaining how the experience of death and loss can be different for children compared with adults. The difference can be in the quality of information children receive, their ability to control events, their previous life experiences and their cognitive level.

Ask the trainees, in pairs, to use this information to consider how their school could help a young person returning after the death or loss of a parent or significant other.

Bring the group back together for a discussion. Write the ideas on the flip chart or whiteboard and then show the trainees Transparency 34. Discuss any differences with the trainees' findings.

Transparencies 35 and 36 show the results from the Operation Iceberg project, and what the bereaved children reported would have helped them at the time of the bereavement. A point to make is that although a large proportion reported that counselling would have helped them, at the time they received no intervention. A low-level intervention such as acknowledgement and listening may have avoided the need for greater intervention.

Transparencies 37 and 38 show the main reactions of children when they attended or did not attend the funeral. The key element seems to be allowing children the choice of whether to attend or not. None of the children who chose to attend felt that there were negative effects. Some of those not allowed to attend did have negative feelings such as regret and feeling excluded from the family. Talk through the main points and distribute Handout 8.

Main points for trainer to emphasise:

1. *Links with the family.* These need to be quickly established, ideally through one 'key person', and regular contact maintained if necessary. The wishes and needs of the family in relation to the loss should be considered.

2. *Key person.* Thought should be given to who should be the key person who makes and keeps contact with the pupil and family.

3. *Communication in school.* Thought needs to be given to how the news of the loss is communicated to both staff and pupils in school. This could take place in assemblies or in class, for example in a 'circle time' activity.

4. *Acknowledgement.* It is important that the young person's loss is acknowledged: for example, simply saying that you are sorry to hear the news of the loss. A more permanent acknowledgement such as a memorial may be appropriate in some circumstances. Sometimes a whole-school acknowledgement, such as an assembly celebrating the life, or representatives from school attending the funeral may be appropriate.

5. *Careful transition.* Consideration needs to be given to the transition of young people back into school. A phased reintroduction to school may be appropriate in some circumstances.

6. *Space to talk.* Give the pupils space to talk but respect the wishes of those who do not wish to talk or who are selective about who they talk to.

7. *Pupil's pace.* It is important that the subject should never be forced on a pupil and that he or she is allowed to take the initiative.

8. *Control and information.* Children often lack both control of things going on in their lives and information as to what is happening.

Close liaison with home is essential to find out what children have been told.

9. *Specialist referral.* Most children, given sensitive support from home and school, will not need specialist referral. In some cases, as mentioned in Chapter 13, it may be necessary to seek further specialist help. Specialist referral may be required in the following circumstances:

- Trauma or violence has been experienced by the pupil.

- Behaviour such as depression or anger becomes extreme or is protracted.

- There is poor attendance at school.

- Grieving is having a significant adverse effect on the pupil's life.

Some of the professionals able to help are listed in Chapter 20. Medical services are usually accessed through the child's GP. Educational services could be accessed directly through established contacts with educational psychologists or educational welfare officers. Agencies in the voluntary sector could be contacted directly.

Materials

- Flip chart or whiteboard and pens

- OHP

- Transparencies 33 to 38

- Handout 8.

Further reading

Holland, J. (2001) *Understanding Children's Experiences of Parental Bereavement.* London: Jessica Kingsley Publishers.

✓

Children are different

- Information

- Control

- Experience

- Cognitive level

- Personality

Helping children

- Links with family

- Key person

- Communication in school

- Acknowledgement

- Careful transition

- Space to talk

- Pupil's pace

- Control and information

- Specialist referral

How schools could have helped

- Listening (49%)

- Counselling (39%)

- Acknowledgement (26%)

- Death education (24%)

- Explanations (16%)

- Telling peers (11%)

✓

What helps?

- Acknowledgement

- Information – child/teachers

- A good listener

- Peer support

✓

Children attending the funeral felt...

- Positive/helped (68%)

- Nothing (24%)

✓

Children not allowed to attend the funeral felt...

- Regret (38%)

- Excluded (19%)

- Angry (13%)

- OK (11%)

- Unsure (8%)

- Protected (3%)

Handout 8: Helping children

- Links with the family need to be very quickly established, ideally through one 'key person' and regular contact maintained if this is thought appropriate. The wishes and needs of the family in relation to the loss need to be considered, especially in terms of their beliefs and what children have been told about the death. The family may also appreciate help and advice at this early time. Research suggests, for example, that children are best given the choice as to whether or not to attend the chapel of rest or funeral. Keeping a scrapbook, memory box or special item belonging to the deceased may help. Other ways of expressing feelings may be through the creative arts. Outside agencies may also be able to support children and the family at this time.

- In some circumstances a whole school acknowledgement, such as an assembly celebrating the life, may be appropriate. Attending the funeral and sending flowers to the family could also be considered.

- The transition of young people back into the school needs to be carefully planned, as it can be a difficult time for youngsters. For some pupils a phased reintroduction to school could be appropriate. Pupils may worry that the surviving parent may also die and this may lead to anxiety concerning separations.

- It is very important that the young person's loss is acknowledged. Simply saying that you were sorry to hear the news of the death may be sufficient. Acknowledgements such as 'I was sorry to hear about…' and 'Would you like to talk about things?' or 'Tell me about it' should help to engage young people. Youngsters should not be pressed to talk, but be given the opportunity to talk to a staff member if they so wish. Pupils may welcome the space to talk, but the wishes of youngsters who do not wish to talk, or who are selective about whom they talk with, should be respected. It is important that the subject should never be forced on pupils and that they are allowed to take the initiative.

- Telling children the truth within the limits of their understanding should help them to gain a better concept of death and would seem to be a better strategy. Young children, for example, may wonder how a heart can be 'attacked', or something as gentle as a 'stroke' can kill. They may be better able to understand that a part of the body has worn out or given a similar explanation.

- Providing information will help young people to avoid building up fantasies and myths around death. These fantasies may well be far worse than the actual reality.

- It is important to liaise closely with the family on this issue and check what the children have been told.

- A more permanent and long-term acknowledgement at school, such as a memorial, may in some circumstances be appropriate on the death of a pupil or staff member, as discussed in Chapter 18.

- Thought needs to be given as to how the news of the loss is communicated to both staff and pupils in school. This could take place at a staff briefing, an assembly or in individual classes. It is important that all the adults at school, including ancillary staff, are aware the pupil has experienced a loss.

- Thought should be given to the possibility of having a key person who makes and keeps contact with the pupil and family.

- Children generally benefit from being given the choice as to whether or not to attend the funeral of a parent.

- Most children, given sensitive support from home and school, will not need specialist referral. In some cases, as mentioned in Chapter 13, it may be necessary to seek further specialist help. This could be the case where the pupil has experienced trauma or violence, or where behaviour such as depression or anger becomes extreme or is protracted. Other warning signs may be poor attendance including truancy or where grieving is having a significant adverse effect on the pupil's life.

- Some of the professionals able to help are listed in Chapter 20. Medical services are usually accessed through the child's GP. Educational services could be accessed directly through established contacts with educational psychologists or educational welfare officers. Agencies in the voluntary sector could be contacted directly.

15

Loss in the curriculum

Introduction

Throughout the school day occasions often arise for formal or informal discussion around the area of loss. Children may talk at school about seeing a hedgehog that had been run over on the road or the death of the class hamster. Taking the opportunity to talk about loss in this informal way is one means of transmitting the values and caring ethos of the school.

Aim

The aim is to give the trainees a greater awareness of how loss and death can be encountered in the curriculum, both formally and informally, planned and serendipitous.

Method of delivery

Ask the trainees to brainstorm the ways in which children may encounter loss and change both in school and at home. Record the replies on a flip chart or whiteboard under the following two headings (Transparencies 39 and 40):

- Informal
- Formal.

Materials

- Flip chart or whiteboard and pens
- OHP
- Transparencies 39 and 40
- Handout 9.

Films/
TV

Local or national
deaths

Informal

Class pets
Plants

School
community
losses

Preparation
for loss

Religious
education

Personal,
social,
health education

Formal

National
Curriculum
science,
history, etc.

Creative art,
music

Handout 9: Loss in the curriculum

Throughout the school day occasions often arise for formal or informal discussion around the area of loss. Children may talk at school about seeing a hedgehog which had been run over on the road or the death of the class hamster. Taking the opportunity to talk about loss in this informal way transmits the implicit values and caring ethos of the school. Some suggested ways of fostering discussion may be through:

- circle time

- tutor time/news time

- peer counselling

- mentoring

- voluntary or staff counsellors.

Loss can be addressed formally through the curriculum in most subject areas, for example:

- Science – the difference between living and non-living

- History – past lives and events

- English – literature, including separation and illness

- PSHE – life skills, relationships and separations

- RE – funerals, rituals and rites associated with different spiritual beliefs

- Music – associated with rites, requiems, meditations.

The temptation in schools may be to focus on the academic content of the subjects, avoiding the potentially more difficult emotional aspects. Simply providing factual knowledge of the funeral rites in the subcontinent of India, for example, may satisfy curriculum requirements but may not engage the pupils at an emotional and personal level. It is important to include the emotional side of any loss. Where teachers encourage openness and reflection, pupils are more likely to develop an awareness of their own feelings and be able to empathise with others.

16

Anticipated and sudden death

Introduction

It is not possible to predict how an individual will respond to any death, but people tend to respond differently depending on whether the death is anticipated or sudden.

Aim

To provide a greater insight into the potential differences between children's responses to sudden and anticipated death.

Method of delivery

Ask the trainees in pairs to consider the two scenarios shown on Transparency 41. This should be photocopied for every trainee.

Ask the trainees to discuss how the two experiences are likely to be different for Lee and for the school. Bring the trainees together in order to brainstorm and discuss their findings. The ideas could be recorded on a flip chart or whiteboard.

Anticipated death – for example, terminal illness

- There is more opportunity for the family and school to prepare than with a sudden death.

- The school can establish early links with the family. Communication can be developed to support the child in school.

- Grieving may relate to the changes caused by the illness.

- The sick person may slowly withdraw from family life as others gradually take on their role. Separation is gradual.

- This is a chance to complete unfinished business and to say goodbye.

Sudden death – for example, road traffic accident

- There is a sudden separation with no warning.

- There may be 'unfinished business' with no chance for the bereaved to say goodbyes.

- The response is reactive rather than proactive.

- The feelings are the same as with any loss but are likely to be more intense and extreme.

- There is no time for preparation by either the school or family so that external support services may not be in place.

Materials

- Flip chart or whiteboard and pens

- OHP

- Transparency 41

- Photocopy of Transparency 41

- Handout 10.

Scenario 1

Lee is an average 13-year-old pupil attending the local secondary school. His mum has just died after a long illness. Lee lives at home with his dad.

Scenario 2

Lee is an average 13-year-old pupil attending the local secondary school. His mum has just died unexpectedly. Lee lives at home with his dad.

Handout 10: Anticipated and sudden death

- It is not possible to make generalisations about a death as each one is individual and unique. However, there are potential differences between anticipated and sudden death which do need consideration.

- There is more opportunity for individuals, the family and the school to prepare for an anticipated death than for a sudden death. The school can establish links with the family and communication can be established to support the child in school before and after the death.

- With anticipated death, the dying person has time to sort out and finalise his or her affairs, with the opportunity of completing any 'unfinished' business. There is also time for goodbyes. The dying person may slowly withdraw from family life as others gradually take on his or her role and the separation is gradual.

- There may also be issues of grieving around any changes caused by the illness. An individual may, for example, become more dependent and lose mobility.

- In contrast, where the death is sudden, there is a separation without warning. Here the dying person will not have had the chance to say goodbye and may have left 'unfinished business'.

- There is no time for preparation by either the individual, family or school, so that the external support services may not be in place. The response here is reactive, at a time of crisis, rather than proactive.

- The feelings are the same as with any loss but are likely to be more intense and extreme in the case of a sudden death.

17

Cultural aspects

Introduction

It is important to be aware that there may be a wide range of beliefs even within families and assumptions should not be made without consultation. The way we perceive death and loss relates not only to ourselves as individuals, but also to our family, community and cultural expectations and experiences. Research indicates that children find active involvement in rites and rituals helpful in their grieving process.

Aim

This is to increase the trainees' awareness of the cultural basis of belief systems. There is the need to develop sensitive communications with the family to establish their beliefs, customs and wishes.

Method of delivery

Ask the trainees in groups of three or four to discuss their own experiences of involvement in the customs, rites and rituals after a death. Ask the trainees to reflect on what they felt helpful and unhelpful.

Next bring the group together and ask the trainees to share their reflections. The trainer should then draw out the similarities and differences of these experiences. Show the trainees Transparency 42, which lists some possible cultural and religious differences.

Materials

- OHP

- Transparency 42

- Handout 11.

Cultural and religious differences

- Grieving response

- Laying out the body

- Viewing the body

- Burial, cremation or other

- Period between death and funeral

- Involvement of women or children

- Beliefs about an afterlife

- Spiritual differences

- Customary mourning period

Handout 11: Cultural aspects

- It is important to be aware that there may be a wide range of beliefs, even within families. Assumptions should not be made without consultation with those involved.

- The way we perceive death and loss relates not only to ourselves as individuals, but also to our family, community and cultural expectations and experiences. The expression of grief may be different in relation to gender, race, culture and ethnicity. The outward expression of grief, such as public wailing, is expected in some cultures, whereas in others this would be regarded as an abnormal response.

- Communication with the family is important and community and religious leaders may also be able to give guidance on rites and customs.

- Research suggests that children generally find active involvement in rites and rituals helpful in their grieving process. It is very important to respect the views and wishes of children and their families.

- There may be differences in how the bereaved initially respond to the death, especially in a public setting. There may be differences as to the 'laying out' of the body and in general the western religions tend to focus on these aspects of how the body is treated. In contrast the eastern religious tend to have more of a focus on the spiritual element.

- The body may be buried, cremated or dealt with in another way. There may be public health issues and legislation that applies in this context.

- There are variations between the period of death and the funeral rites, in terms of both timing and also who has access to the body. At times women and children may be excluded from contact with the body, as may others not sharing the same belief.

- Belief in an afterlife or not will vary and there may be other spiritual differences. The period of mourning may vary and may be quite prescriptive as to rites and rituals.

- Further information is best sought locally from:

  - the family
  - community and religious leaders
  - local authority departments
  - Citizens Advice Bureaux
  - local interest groups
  - library information
  - directories.

18

Death of a pupil or staff member

Introduction

The death of a member of the school community may have a significant impact on many. As with any death it should be sensitively approached. Other relevant chapters include Chapter 10 on children's understanding of death and potential reactions and Chapter 19 on policies.

Aim

This is to help the trainees gain a greater awareness of the issues surrounding the death of a member of the school community.

Method of delivery

Ask pairs of trainees to consider the scenario on a handout copied from Transparency 43. Ask the trainees to write their responses to the following questions on a large sheet of paper and after ten minutes bring their ideas back to the group as a whole. These could be recorded on a flip chart or whiteboard. Then show the trainees Transparency 44, which gives some of the things to be considered generally when breaking the news of a death in the school community. The following should be given prior consideration:

1. It is important that clear factual information is provided as quickly as possible to avoid rumours developing. There may be a profound grief reaction by both pupils and staff, in particular at any large-scale gathering where the news is announced. The news may best be delivered in tutor or class groups, with awareness that some may become extremely distressed. Ideally individuals should receive help from those whom they know. The role of outside agencies may be to help teachers to support pupils rather than in direct work. Staff too may need support. Most individuals, given sensitive support from home and school, will not need specialist referral. In

some cases, as mentioned in Chapter 13 on learning and behaviour, it may be necessary to seek further specialist help. This could be the case where behaviour such as depression or anger becomes extreme or is protracted. Other signs are where there is poor attendance or where grieving is having a significant adverse effect on the individual's life. Some of the professionals able to help are listed in Chapter 20. Parents need to know what pupils have been told about the death and surrounding circumstances and this should be by means of a special letter home. This could include a list of books and a key person for parents to contact if further help is needed.

2.   There may be involvement of the media and a key person needs to be identified to liaise with them and to inform the governors and local education authority, who may be able to offer support. The family also needs to be consulted and, where possible, to agree with any statement which is issued.

3.   Consideration of the appropriateness of an immediate event of public recognition such as an assembly.

4.   Consideration of a memorial such as the planting of a tree.

5.   There may be an element of trauma if, for example, the death was witnessed by pupils or staff. This could be the case whether the death is by accident or natural causes such as a heart attack. Help here could be sought from agencies such as counsellors or psychologists.

Materials

- Flip chart or whiteboard and pens
- OHP
- Transparencies 43 and 44
- Photocopy of Transparency 43
- Handout 12.

A Death in the school community

Colin had been a popular teacher in a large primary school for the past eight years. He was killed in a road traffic accident on his way to school, not seen by any of the school community. The school was told by a close relative.

- Who should break the news in school?

- How and where should the news be broken?

- What reactions may be anticipated?

- What short- or long-term responses should be anticipated?

Response to a death in the school community

- Allocate a key person

- Consider how and where to break news

- Give clear factual information quickly

- Anticipate and plan for distress

- Know how to access outside agencies

- Support staff as well as pupils

- Plan for links with media and LEA

- Send explanatory letters to all parents

- Celebrate the life

- If traumatic death, refer to outside agencies

Handout 12: Death of a pupil or staff member

1. The immediate need will be to obtain clear factual information and to communicate this news to both staff and pupils. A link needs to be quickly established and maintained with the family of the deceased to provide support and determine their wishes.

2. It is important that the news of the death is broken to others in a sensitive manner.

3. Ideally a plan should be in place to cope with instances that link with the school's emergency disaster response plan. Teachers need to be aware of the details of any such plan. There may be an element of trauma if, for example, the death was witnessed by pupils or staff. This could be the case whether the death is by accident or from natural causes such as a heart attack. Help here could be sought from agencies such as counsellors or psychologists.

4. It is important that information is provided as quickly as possible to avoid rumours developing. There may be a profound grief reaction displayed by both pupils and staff, in particular at any large-scale gathering where the news is announced. Some individuals, both staff and pupils, may become distressed by the news and there needs to be a plan for their support.

5. The news of the death may best be delivered to the staff in a briefing and to pupils in tutor or class groups. Support staff should also be informed as should outside agencies visiting the school. Ideally individuals should receive both the news and support from those whom they know well. The role of outside agencies may be to help teachers to support pupils rather than in direct work.

6. Staff too may need support to deal both with their own feelings and emotions as well as with the additional stress of supporting colleagues and pupils. This aspect may easily be overlooked.

7. In some circumstances the media may become involved and a key person needs to be identified to liaise with them and to inform the governors and local education authority (LEA), who may be able to offer support. The family also needs to be consulted and, where possible, to agree with any statement which is issued to the media.

8. Most individuals, given sensitive support from home and school, will not need a specialist referral. In some cases, as mentioned in Chapter 13 on learning and behaviour, it may be necessary to seek further specialist help. Some of the professionals able to help are listed in Chapter 20. These may be needed where:

    - depression or anger becomes extreme or is protracted
    - there is poor attendance at school
    - grieving has a significant adverse effect on the individual's life.

9. All parents need to know what pupils have been told about the death and the surrounding circumstances and this information could be sent home in a special letter. This could also include a list of useful books and a key person for parents to contact if further help is needed.

10. An immediate event of public recognition, such as an assembly, may be appropriate and consideration could be given to a lasting memorial such as the planting of a tree or garden seat. A memory and condolence book may also be appropriate.

19

Loss response policies

Introduction

There is a debate as to whether or not schools should establish proactive policies in relation to loss. A reason often given for not having a policy is that as each loss is unique, then an individual response is required and therefore a general policy would not help. Each bereavement is unique, but there are common factors and it is possible to produce a checklist as a reminder of things that may need consideration. This checklist could be discussed by all the staff at a time of calm rather than in crisis after a death.

Aim

This aim is to consider the advantages of having a proactive policy in the area of loss and to consider the content of such a policy.

Method of delivery

Ask pairs of trainees to consider items they would include on a checklist in a loss response policy. Ask the trainees to write their ideas on a large sheet of paper and after ten minutes bring their ideas back to the group as a whole.

Then show the trainees Transparency 45, which gives some of the items that could be included in a checklist.

Materials

- Flip chart or whiteboard and pens

- OHP

- Transparency 45

- Handout 13.

Policy checklist

- Allocate key person

- Liaise with family

- Establish facts

- Inform staff

- Inform pupils

- Attend funeral/send flowers

- Offer support if needed

- Monitor return to school

- Monitor and review response

Handout 13: Loss response policies

- It can be debated as to whether or not schools should establish proactive policies in relation to loss. A reason often given for not having a policy is that as each loss is unique, then an individual response is required and a general policy would not help.

- Each bereavement is unique, but there are common factors and it is possible to produce a checklist as a reminder of things that may need consideration. This checklist could be discussed by all the school staff at a time of calm rather than in crisis after a death.

- As each school is set in a different context it is not possible to provide a definitive policy for all schools. This would not be desirable and the policy should be a 'living document' and one to which all the staff are able to contribute. The immediate need will be to obtain clear factual information and to communicate this news to both staff and pupils.

- A policy and plan could include a strategy for establishing links with the family, and a key person to liaise with the family may be helpful. This could help to establish the facts and also the wishes of the family. There may be an initial response in visiting the family, sending flowers or attending the funeral. The family could be offered support or advice if needed.

- Consideration needs to be given as to how to inform staff and pupils at school, as well as parents, if this is thought necessary.

- Care needs to be taken with the transition of a bereaved pupil back into school. Opportunity to talk with a staff member may be very helpful. The response should be monitored and evaluated, which may lead to a possible revision of the policy in the school.

20

Helping agencies

Introduction

There is a variety of agencies able to offer support to both schools and individuals who have experienced bereavement.

Aim

The aim is to alert the trainees to the various agencies able to offer support.

Method of delivery

Circulate the handout of the national and local contact lists to the trainees. This could be done towards the end of the session. Any known local contacts could be provided and the trainees could be given five minutes to read through the agencies and to make further suggestions. These could then be shared with the rest of the group.

Materials

- Handout 14 – please insert local contacts
- Handout 15.

Handout 14: Local contact list

Citizens Advice Bureau

Department of Social Security

Educational psychology service

Educational welfare officers

Education authority

General practitioners

Health authority

Clinical psychologists

Child psychiatrists

Psychiatric nurses

Ministers of religion

School nurses

School counsellors

Social services

Local hospice

Local Cruse Bereavement Care

Local Samaritans

Local undertakers

Others

Handout 15: National contact list

Child Bereavement Network
8 Wakley Street
London EC1V 7QE
Tel: 020 7843 6309

A national multi-agency forum in the area of child bereavement, hosted by the NCB.

Child Bereavement Trust
Harleyford Estate
Henley Road
Marlow, Bucks SL7 2DX
Tel: 01494 678088

The Trust has a useful publications and information service.

Compassionate Friends
53 North Street
Bristol BS3 1EN
Tel: 01179 665202

Compassionate Friends offers support for parents who have experienced the death of a child.

Cruse Bereavement Care
Cruse House
126 Sheen Road
Richmond, Surrey TW9 1UR
Tel: 020 8939 9530

Cruse is the national organisation for the bereaved and their children. Local Cruse contacts will be able to offer counselling for adults, but not necessarily for children. They will be able to suggest where counselling for children can be obtained.

Hospice Information
St Christopher's Hospice
51–9 Lawrie Park Road
London SE26 6DZ
Tel: 0870 903 3903

National Association of Bereavement Services
20 Norton Folgate
London E1 6DB
Tel: 020 7247 1080 (24 hours)

A directory of bereavement services throughout the UK is being compiled.

National Association of Citizens' Advice Bureaux
Myddleton House
115–23 Pentonville Road
London N1 9LZ
Tel: 020 7833 2181

CABs are a useful source of information about who can help.

National Association of Funeral Directors
618 Warwick Road
Solihull, West Midlands B91 1AA
Tel: 0121 711 1343

Samaritans
10 The Grove
Slough SL1 1QP
Tel: 01753 532713

The Samaritans offer support to people who feel isolated, desperate or suicidal. There are branches throughout the UK and a 24-hour free and confidential service.

Winston's Wish
Gloucestershire Royal Hospital
Great Western Road
Gloucester GL1 3NN
Tel: 01452 394377

This is a grief support programme for children.

Information in relation to ethnic minorities and religions can be sought nationally or locally from:

- community and religious leaders
- local authority departments
- national government departments
- Citizens Advice Bureaux
- local interest groups
- libraries
- local and national directories
- World Wide Web.

21
Resources

Introduction

There is a variety of useful books available for both children and adults that offer further insights into the experience of loss and bereavement.

Aim

This is to alert the trainees to other useful publications.

Method of delivery

Circulate Handout 16 to the trainees. It would be helpful if a selection of the books listed or others found to be useful could also be shown to the trainees. This could take place towards the end of the course. The trainees could be given a few minutes to read through the list and look at the books. The group could then be called together to share ideas and suggestions.

Materials

- Handout 16
- Books as available.

Handout 16: Reading lists

Reading list for younger children

Alex, M. and Alex, B. (1983) *Grandpa and Me.* Oxford: Lion.

Althea and Sarah Wimperis (2001) *When Uncle Bob Died.* London: Usborne.

Birmingham, J. (2003) *Grandpa.* Harmondsworth: Puffin.

Carle, E. (1994) *The Very Hungry Caterpillar.* London: Hamilton.

Clardy, A.F. (1984) *Dusty Was My Friend: Coming to Terms with Loss.* New York: Human Sciences Press.

Cowlishaw, S. and Cathy Gale (1993) *When My Little Sister Died.* New York: Merlin.

Limb, S. and Munoz, C. (1995) *Come Back, Grandma.* London: Red Fox.

Lorentzen, K. (1983) *LankyLonglegs.* London: Dent.

Madler, T. (1995) *Why Did Grandma Die?* Oxford: Blackwell.

St Christopher's Hospice (1989) *Someone Special has Died.* London: St Christopher's Hospice.

Stickney, D. (1997) *Waterbugs and Dragonflies.* London: Continuum.

Varley, S (1992) Badger's Parting Gifts. London: Andersen Press.

Viorst, J. (1987) *The Tenth Good Thing about Barney.* London: HarperCollins.

White, E.B. (1993) *Charlotte's Web.* Harmondsworth: Puffin.

Reading list for older children

Branfield, J. (1992) *Fox in Winter.* New York: Atheneum.

Buchanan Smith, B. (1992) *A Taste of Blackberries.* Harmondsworth: Penguin.

Hollins, S. and Sireling, L. (2004) *When Dad Died.* London: Gaskell.

Hollins, S. and Sireling, L. (2004) *When Mum Died.* London: Gaskell.

Hoy, L. (1987) *Your Friend, Rebecca.* London: Random House.

Hunter, M. (1972) *A Sound of Chariots.* London: Hamilton Armada.

Little, J. (1985) *Mama's Going to Buy You a Mockingbird.* Harmondsworth: Penguin.

Lowry, L. (1984) *A Summer to Die.* New York: Laweleaf.

St Christopher's Hospice (1989) *Someone Special Has Died.* London: St Christopher's Hospice.

St Christopher's Hospice (1991) *Your Parent has Died.* London: St Christopher's Hospice.

Steffes, D. (1997) *When Someone Dies: How Schools Can Help Bereaved Students.* Richmond: Cruse.

Zindel, B. and Zindel, P. (1998) *A Star for the Latecomer.* London: Random House.

Reading list for adults

Bending, M. (1993) *Caring for Bereaved Children.* Richmond: Cruse.

Chadwick, A. (1994) *Living with Grief in School: Guidance for Primary School Teachers.* Biggin Hill: Family Reading Centre.

Dyregrov, A. (1990) *Grief in Children: A Handbook for Adults.* London: Jessica Kingsley Publishers.

Fisher, M. and Kassell, C. (1989) *A Child's Questions about Death.* Preston: St Catherine's Hospice.

Goldman, L. (1999) *Life and Loss.* London: Accelerated Development.

Grollman, E.A. (1993) *Straight Talk about Death to Teenagers.* Manchester: Thanatos.

Holland, J. (1997) *Coping with Bereavement: A Handbook for Teachers.* Cardiff: Cardiff Academic Press.

Holland, J. (2001) *Understanding Children's Experiences of Parental Bereavement.* London: Jessica Kingsley Publishers.

Klass, D., Silverman, P.R. and Nickman, S.L. (1996) *Continuing Bonds: New Understandings of Grief.* London: Taylor & Francis.

Kübler-Ross, E. (1980) *On Death and Dying.* London: Tavistock/Routledge.

Leaman, O. (1995) *Compassionate Approaches in the Classroom.* London: Cassell.

Parkes, C.M. (1975) *Studies of Grief in Adult Life.* Harmondsworth: Penguin.

Turner, M. (1998) *Talking with Children and Young People about Death and Dying.* London: Jessica Kingsley Publishers.

Yule, W. and Gold, A. (1995) *Wise before the Event: Coping with Crises in Schools.* London; Calouste Gulbenkian Foundation.

Ward, B. (1996) *Good Grief 1: Exploring Feelings, Loss and Death with Under Elevens.* London: Jessica Kingsley Publishers.

Ward, B. (1996) *Good Grief 2: Exploring Feelings, Loss and Death with Over Elevens and Adults.* London: Jessica Kingsley Publishers.

Worden, J.W. (1991) *Grief Counselling and Grief Therapy.* London: Tavistock/ Routledge.

NOTES

NOTES

also published by JKP
Supporting Children in Public Care in Schools
A Resource for Trainers of Teachers, Carers and Social Workers

John Holland and Catherine Randerson

ISBN 184310 325 7 (paperback) 144 pages

Supporting Children in Public Care in Schools is a resource for anyone involved in training teachers, social workers, carers and all those who support young people in public care.

Based on collaborative multi-agency and multi-professional work with psychologists, teachers, social workers and nurses, it focuses on the different types of loss that children in care may experience, such as the loss of family, of routine, of hobbies or of physical affection. The training pack includes photocopiable material and instructions for more than a dozen training sessions. These address a range of issues, including the reasons why young people are in care, how feelings of loss relate to the experience of being in care, and how being in care may affect education, attainment and emotional attachment. There is also a focus on making school transitions work effectively by ensuring a positive welcoming ethos and good communication within the school.

The flexible modular structure of this resource means that sessions can be planned around trainee's needs and can be delivered as single topics if required. Each training module includes group activities, templates for OHP transparencies, handouts for trainees and a bibliography.

This much-needed training package raises awareness of the experiences of young people in public care and provides essential guidance for staff in schools or other settings on how to assist young people through corporate parenting, smooth transitions into school, designated teachers and personal education plans.

John Holland works at Hull City Psychological Service. He is an educational psychologist, having previously worked as an infant and special needs teacher. He is the author of *Lost for Words* and *Understanding Children's Experiences of Parental Bereavement*, also published by Jessica Kingsley Publishers, and numerous articles on childhood bereavement. **Catherine Randerson** works for the Interagency Link Team, Hull.

Contents: 1. Introduction. 2. Introducing course members to the package. 3. Ethos. 4. Icebreakers. 5. Research base. 6. Corporate parenting. 7. Why young people are in public care. 8. Young people in public care, attainments and attendance. 9. The experience of being in public care. 10. Loss experience. 11. Attachment. 12. Changes in learning and behaviour. 13. Young people as individuals. 14. Helping young people. 15. The designated teacher. 16. Personal education plans (PEPs). 17. 'Jargon busting'.

To order a copy of *Supporting Children in Public Care in Schools*, please visit www.jkp.com or contact us:
Jessica Kingsley Publishers, 116 Pentonville Road, London N1 9JB, UK
Tel: +44 (0)20 7833 2307
Fax: +44 (0)20 7837 2917
Email: post@jkp.com